I0820422

POLITICAL SYSTEMS IN ACTION

PARLIAMENTARY GOVERNMENT

From the Viking Althing to Modern Parliament

ALEX WEBB

CHERITON
CHILDREN'S BOOKS

Published in 2025 by **Cheriton Children's Books**
1 Bank Drive West, Shrewsbury, Shropshire, SY3 9DJ, UK

First Edition

Author: Alex Webb
Designer: Paul Myerscough
Editor: Sarah Eason
Proofreader: Anna Chambers

Picture credits: Cover: Doodle Press. Inside: p4: Shutterstock/Fred Duval, p5: Shutterstock/Rambleon, p6: Shutterstock/David JC, p7: Shutterstock/Philip Bird LRPS CPAGB, p8: Wikimedia Commons/James William Edmund Doyle, p9: Wikimedia Commons/Foreign and Commonwealth Office, p10: Shutterstock/Olavs, p11: Shutterstock/Wangkun Jia, p12: Shutterstock/StreetVJ, p13t: Shutterstock/PradeepGaurs, p13b: Shutterstock/Arindam Banerjee, p14: Shutterstock/Penofoto, p15l: Shutterstock/Michael Tubi, p15r: Shutterstock/Frederic Legrand/COMEO, p16t: Wikimedia Commons/UK Parliament/Maria Unger, p16b: Shutterstock/Brian Duffy, p17: Shutterstock/ITS, p18: Wikimedia Commons/Myrabella, p19: Shutterstock/Traveller70, p20: Shutterstock/Alessia Pierdomenico, p21: Shutterstock/Photocosmos1, p22: Shutterstock/Sean Aidan Calderbank, p23: Shutterstock/David Fowler, p24: Shutterstock/Chris Dorney, p25: Wikimedia Commons/Yousuf Karsh, p26: Shutterstock/Drop of Light, p27: Wikimedia Commons/Mark Tantrum, p28: Shutterstock/Chameleons Eye, p29: Shutterstock/Paparazzza, p30: Shutterstock/Heide Pinkall, p31: Wikimedia Commons/UK House of Lords, p32: Shutterstock/Michel Loiselle, p33: Shutterstock/Art Babych, p34: Shutterstock/Chris Dorney, p35: Shutterstock/TX King, p36: Shutterstock/Sumit Saraswat, p37: Shutterstock/Katherine Welles, p38: Shutterstock/Török Csaba, p39: Shutterstock/Mike Dotta, p40: Wikimedia Commons/Prime Minister's Office, Government of India, p41: Shutterstock, p42: Shutterstock/Photocosmos1, p43: Flickr/Keir Starmer, p44: Shutterstock/Gareth Willey, p45: Wikimedia Commons.

Printed in the United States of America

Contents

CHAPTER 1

The Story of Parliamentary Government

The parliamentary system is one of the oldest forms of government. The system evolved from ancient Greek democracies and monarchies, when kings and queens ruled kingdoms. The parliamentary system was very different from the single rule of a king or queen—it involved the people in the rule of their country. Today, it is a system that many countries have adopted and under which they also thrive.

A Democratic System

A parliamentary system of government is a democracy, just like the presidential system of the United States. A democracy is a type of government in which a country's people take part. They choose their leaders, and those leaders create laws to rule the country. Laws are the authority in a democracy. A country's laws, system of government, and protection of human rights are defined in its constitution.

In the British parliamentary system, the prime minister is the leader of the political party that won the election. The current prime minister is Sir Keir Starmer, shown here with his wife Victoria.

Parliament Hill is home to Canada's government, where members of parliament gather to make laws.

Comparing Systems

In a presidential system, a president is the head of state and the head of government. In a parliamentary system, two different people have these roles. The head of state is the highest-ranked person in a country. The head of government is the chief executive, who is involved with making laws and running the country. The people of a country do not choose the head of government. This person is the leader of the political party that wins the election, after the people have voted.

A System of Chambers

A parliament can either be bicameral or unicameral. A bicameral system has two legislative, or law-making, chambers. A unicameral system has one legislative, or law-making, chamber. Canada has a bicameral system, with two legislative chambers: the Senate and the House of Commons. Members elected by the people make up the House of Commons, while the head of state appoints senate members.

PARLIAMENTARY GOVERNMENT: PAST AND PRESENT

In this book we will look at the political system of parliamentary government, its history, and its place in the world today. We'll compare parliamentary government past with parliamentary government present, and look at some of the key figures of this political system in the People and Politics features. Look out too for the Parliamentary Government in Action features throughout the book and try to answer the questions that accompany some of them.

An Ancient Start

The ancient Greeks developed democratic governments around 500 BCE. This early form of democracy included three institutions—the assembly, which made decisions about war and foreign policy, a Council of Five Hundred, which made decisions about how to govern, and the courts, with juries of citizens, which upheld the law. This system survived for 200 years. It would not catch on in other countries until centuries later.

This is a statue of Alfred the Great, showing him as a triumphant king. Alfred was famous for protecting his people from violent Viking raids and also introducing a system of law and order.

PEOPLE AND POLITICS

Alfred the Great (849–899) was an Anglo-Saxon ruler in ninth-century Britain. He defended his small kingdom from the Vikings and went on to rule over a great area of land. His united tribes were called the "Angles," and over time this word became the "English." Alfred encouraged people to learn and created laws that were intended to be fair to everyone. His rule saw people belonging not just to a tribe but to a wide area of land ruled by one leader (who would eventually be the king of England).

The Modern System

The modern parliamentary system has roots in the medieval period, from around 500 to 1500 CE. The first parliament was the Althing, in Iceland, around 930. Even earlier than this, a parliamentary democracy began to form in England, which was not a united country at the time, but was made up of communities, or kingdoms. The ruling kings sometimes held meetings—called the Witan—with advisors and nobles, to discuss important community matters. The Witan also met to discuss matters of war and peace treaties between warring parties.

Seeking Advice

The king made the laws, but needed the advice, and support, of community leaders to make them work. These advising groups became more permanent from the eleventh century. The groups worked to help the king govern the country and decide important matters that affected its future. A larger group of advising noblemen—the Great Council—became the basis for the United Kingdom's (UK's) House of Lords. Today, the House of Lords is one of the two legislative chambers in the UK parliament system.

The First Parliament

For local matters, the moot was an assembly where local cases were heard, and judgments made. Important local people, such as sheriffs, lords, bishops, and village representatives, heard the cases, and made decisions. At this time, England began to be divided into areas, called counties, so each moot became the County Court and formed the basis for the legislative chamber, which is called the House of Commons. The Great Council and the County Courts began to meet in the thirteenth century. This was the first English parliament—a meeting of the lords, noblemen, and the representatives of local people.

Moot Hall in Aldeburgh, UK, was built in the sixteenth century, and is still used for town council meetings today.

Early Kingdoms

The early kingdoms of England later joined together with one ruling king. The first gatherings of nobles and local representatives did not happen regularly, only when the king called upon the groups to meet. The king also did not legally have to do anything that was discussed at the meetings. Unhappy with this, the lords forced the king to agree to the Magna Carta (meaning Great Charter), in 1215. This document became very important to the development of modern democracies. It listed the rights of the people and forced the king to listen to and follow the lords' advice.

A Model Parliament

In 1275, the first parliament was held that included elected representatives from each county, and city or town. The next such meeting, known as the Model Parliament, was held in 1295. The system continued to develop into the next century, and from January 1327 onward, the parliament always included elected representatives. The government of England had formed into three bodies: monarch, lords, and the commons. These three bodies would develop into the current parliamentary system in the UK. This system of government did not remain only in the UK, however.

PEOPLE AND POLITICS

King John of England was not popular during his rule (1199–1216). His costly battles lost a lot of land to France. The lords were paying the most for these wars in taxes and they rebelled, forcing John to sign the Magna Carta in 1215. New taxes could only be passed with the lords' permission and a council of 25 lords was formed to monitor the king's rule.

The signing of the Magna Carta has been an inspiration for many paintings since the act.

The Magna Carta has roused interest around the world. This exhibition in Beijing, China, drew crowds of people who came to learn more about the document.

Parliamentary Government in Action

The Magna Carta is very important to democratic governments around the world. It was one of the first documents that defined the rights of a country's people. Here is a quote from the Magna Carta:

> "No freeman shall be taken, imprisoned, disseised [have their land stolen], outlawed, banished, or in any way destroyed, nor will We [the king] proceed against or prosecute him, except by the lawful judgment of his peers and by the law of the land."

Compare this with a quote from the US Bill of Rights, which was inspired by the Magna Carta: "No person shall … be deprived of life, liberty, or property, without due process of law." Consider how these quotes are similar and how they are different.

Does reading a quote from the Magna Carta help you understand why it was important in establishing the parliamentary system in the UK? If so, how?

The Palace of Westminster is home to the British Parliament in London, UK.

Other Parliamentary Systems

England's parliament is just one example of the development of parliamentary governments in Europe. Similar systems have grown in many other European countries. Sweden's parliament was established in 1809, and, soon after, the Netherlands, Norway, Denmark, and Belgium, and other northern and western European nations, had a parliamentary system. The popularity of the parliamentary system grew and today, more than 20 countries in this part of the world are organized by parliamentary forms of government.

Following a New Order

Although the different parliaments across Europe developed in their own ways, they eventually included representation of people from different social and economic classes. These parliaments also marked a change from a monarch's complete power over government. Where there was a parliament, a monarch had to make decisions with the people of the country they ruled. The parliamentary system that developed in England, and later the UK, was the system that many countries adopted. It is called the Westminster system.

Once an Empire

The UK once had a much larger world influence than it does today—during the time of the British Empire, which lasted from the seventeenth to the twentieth centuries. The Empire had settlements and colonies in many parts of the world, including Africa, the Caribbean, Asia, and also the colonies of America.

Leaving and Staying

Some countries, such as Ireland and America, gained their independence from the British Empire through wars. Other countries, such as Canada, Australia, and New Zealand, became independent nations, but kept ties with the UK. They later formed part of the British Commonwealth. Although they are independent nations, they have kept the British monarchy as their head of state.

Royal tours are often popular in many Commonwealth countries such as Canada.

Parliamentary Government in Action

The British Empire may not exist anymore, but many former colonies— now Commonwealth countries—have adopted a parliamentary system based on the Westminster model.

Why do you think these countries have this system of government?

How do you think the British Empire helped spread this system of government around the world?

PAST AND PRESENT:

Many countries that were formerly part of the British Empire feel that they were exploited under the Empire and are owed an apology by Britain for acts carried out during the time of British rule. Do you think Britain owes an apology to nations around the world? Which nations do you think are most in need of apology and reparation?

Parliaments Around the World

While there are many countries throughout Europe that have a parliamentary system of government, other parts of the world have also adopted this system. Today, 190 countries have a national parliament. It is the most common form of government in Europe, and is also common in the Caribbean and other areas that once formed the British Empire.

PEOPLE AND POLITICS

In Japan, the emperor is a hereditary monarch. Naruhito came to the throne in 2019 when his 85-year-old father abdicated. As emperor, Naruhito is the ceremonial head of state, and he appoints a prime minister to lead the country. He performs some duties with the advice and approval of his cabinet.

Emperor Naruhito and his wife, Masako, on the day of his ascension in 2019

The Indian parliament meets in Parliament House, New Delhi.

Adopting the System

Many African and Asian countries have adopted the parliamentary system. Lesotho and Mauritius, two former British colonies in Africa, use that system of government, as does Ethiopia. India, once part of the British Empire, introduced a parliamentary system in 1947. It has a president as head of state, a prime minister as head of government, and two legislative houses: the Rajya Sabha (Council of States) and Lok Sabha (House of the People).

Thailand established a parliament in 1992. Japan also has a parliamentary system, established in 1946, with the emperor of Japan as its head of state. In the Oceania region of the southwest Pacific Ocean, Australia, New Zealand, and Papua New Guinea also have parliamentary systems. New Zealand's formed in 1853, Australia's in 1901, and Papua New Guinea's as recently as 1975.

All Part of the Commonwealth

Canada established its parliamentary system in 1867. In the Caribbean and Central America, 11 countries also have parliaments, including Antigua, Bahamas, Barbados, Dominica, and Jamaica. All these countries are part of the British Commonwealth and adopted the Westminster system when they became independent nations. Parliamentary governments have been established around the world. From its roots in the UK to the world, the parliamentary system remains a governmental system that works for many countries.

Justin Trudeau is the current prime minister of Canada. The country established its parliamentary system in 1867.

CHAPTER 2

Understanding Parliamentary Systems

Different parliaments around the world vary in how they operate. These differences have developed according to the history and needs of each country. All countries that have a parliament have assemblies of representatives and executive branches. There are three defining characteristics of all parliamentary systems: head of state, head of government, and executive branch.

A Separate Role

The role of the head of state is separate from that of the head of government. The head of state is a patriotic and ceremonial representative of the country. This person may be the most important in the whole country, but they do not have power to make political decisions. The head of state can be a president or a monarch.

A cabinet is formed by the head of government in a parliamentary system. The cabinet is a group of advisors who are appointed to help the head of government run the country. This photograph shows the German cabinet at a meeting in 2022.

Parliamentary Government in Action

A monarch is a king or queen, who passes the title down through their family. A parliamentary republic does not have a monarch as its head of state. Instead, a president fills this role. The people of a country with a monarch have no say in choosing that person, but the people of a republic can elect their president. While parliaments may change every few years, monarchs remain in their roles, sometimes for decades.

What do you think is the advantage of having a monarch as the head of state?

What do you think is the advantage of having a president as the head of state?

King Charles III (left) is the head of state in the UK, which is a monarchy. President Emannuel Macron (right) is the head of state in France, which is a republic.

Forming a Government

The head of state appoints the head of government. The head of government is the leader of the political party that has the most support in the main assembly once all the members of that assembly have been voted in during an election. The head of government forms the government by choosing a group of trusted advisors—the cabinet—from other members of parliament. This group forms the executive branch.

Making the Law

The people who make up the executive branch are chosen from members of the assembly. They are the top leaders of the government and have the job of drawing up, and implementing, the changes and laws that they want to make. They are responsible to and need the support of the assembly. We will look at the defining structure of the UK parliament, to understand better how a parliamentary government works.

In the UK

Just like other democratic bodies, parliaments are arranged to divide power between different groups of people. This ensures that no one branch of government has too much power over a country. The UK parliament is made up of three branches: the executive (the people who make the government), the legislature (parliament itself), and the judiciary (the courts).

Sir Keir Starmer is shown here leading a debate in the House of Commons.

The Structure of Power

The executive branch contains the monarch, the prime minister (the head of government), the cabinet, and support staff called civil servants. The prime minister chooses 20 or more trusted advisors to form the cabinet, taken from members of the two legislative bodies. Together, they form the government. It is the job of the government to run a country according to its existing laws and to propose new laws when needed.

Two Houses

The UK parliament has two legislative bodies—the House of Commons and the House of Lords. The Commons has over 600 members, elected by the public. The Lords has more than 700 members, appointed by the head of state. Together, they make laws and examine the actions of the government. They also debate, or talk through, issues that are important to the country.

The UK judiciary includes judges, shown here, who work with juries and other members of the judiciary system to enforce law and deliver punishments in the form of sentences.

A System of Courts

The judiciary branch is made up of the courts of the UK, and includes the Supreme Court, the Court of Appeal, and the High Court. It also includes the Regional and District Courts. It is the job of this branch to decide whether the laws of the country are just and are being appropriately followed by the people.

A parliamentary government is a democracy that is ruled by its people. Citizens of the country elect members of parliament (MPs) during elections, to represent their area of the country. It is also the job of MPs to vote for or against laws on behalf of the people they represent.

Kemi Badenoch is the MP for North West Essex, England.

Parliamentary Government in Action

A country's constitution is a document that sets out the rules for governing that country. The British constitution dates back to around 1066. It is an evolving document that was meant to be amended and changed throughout the centuries. These changes are made through Acts of Parliament.

PAST AND PRESENT:

A "living constitution" is one that naturally evolves over time without having to be formally amended. Judges have the final say over how a constitution should be interpreted. What are the challenges of this system in a rapidly changing world?

How do you think the system of a living constitution may need to be adapted to deal with modern society?

Rules of Government

A parliamentary democracy is based on its country's constitution. This document defines where certain powers lie within a country, how they are constructed, and how they operate. It also defines the rights of a country's people. That means a people's basic rights and freedoms. A constitution does not set out how the government works in a practical way, however. Instead, those working systems evolve over time during the course of each government.

An Ancient System

In the UK, the constitution dates to around 1066, when the Normans invaded and conquered England. It is an ever-evolving set of rules. Unlike the United States, the UK does not have this set out in an actual document, but has what is sometimes called an "unwritten constitution." For example, it is not written anywhere that the prime minister must be chosen from the House of Commons. Yet, this has become common practice in the UK government. Most younger countries have written constitutions. This is because one had to be created when the country was formed.

PEOPLE AND POLITICS

When the Norman invader William the Conqueror (c.1028–1087) defeated England's King Harold II at the Battle of Hastings in 1066, he found ways to take control of this new land and its people. He gave large areas of land to the nobles, in return for their support in raising money and an army. This was important to the development of constitutional government—an example of those in power pledging to respect the rights of the people who gave them allegiance.

This famous tapestry, known as the Bayeaux Tapestry, shows the defeat of Harold II at the Battle of Hastings in 1066.The new king, William the Conqueror, made radical changes to the way that England was ruled.

William the Conqueror

Parliamentary Government in Action

"A constitution is not the act of a government, but of a people constituting a government; and government without a constitution, is power without a right."

These words were written in 1791 by Thomas Paine (1737–1809), one of the founding fathers of the United States, in his book *The Rights of Man*.

What do you think Paine means by "government without a constitution, is power without a right?"

Not Above the Law

Originating in the political world of ancient Greece, the "rule of law" is a very old principle of great importance to the UK Constitution. It means that no one is above the law of a country, which is a basic principle of most civilized societies. It signifies, too, that a country's people, its rulers, and its government are all subject to the laws of that country. A parliament is expected to observe the rule of law as part of the democratic process.

The Chief Power

A prime minister is the chief executive power in a parliamentary system. Instead of being directly elected by the people, as a president is, a prime minister is chosen from the members of the elected legislature. One party usually has the majority in the legislature, and the leader of that party will be the prime minister. The prime minister will also serve as an elected MP.

Italian prime minister, Giorgia Meloni, answers questions during a meeting of parliament in 2024

The Role of Prime Minister

A prime minister oversees the laws proposed by the government and passed by parliament. They appoint judges and other government posts, and are responsible for all the agencies and civil servants who run the affairs of government. In the UK, the prime minister regularly meets with the monarch, who is allowed to express their own views and give advice, but must not try to influence how the government acts.

Parliamentary Government in Action

In the UK parliament, Prime Minister's Questions (PMQs) is a weekly event. Fifteen questions are chosen for members of parliament to put to the prime minister, as well as questions from the leaders of opposition parties. The prime minister doesn't know what questions will be asked but is highly briefed by advisors ahead of time.

Why do you think PMQs is important to parliamentary democracy?

How might PMQs affect the credibility of a prime minister and the loyalty of his supporters?"

Daily Duties of a Prime Minister

The prime minister is actively involved with the business of the legislature. During parliamentary sessions, this involves making formal announcements, answering questions from members of parliament, and taking part in debates in the House of Commons. These duties are also shared with the cabinet, which helps the prime minister make government decisions.

Not Without Support

The prime minister is accountable to the UK parliament and needs the support of the majority of its members. If members of parliament have serious doubts about the current prime minister and the government, the members can cast a vote of "no confidence." If, after 14 days, the parliament still has no confidence in the government, a general, or national, election is held to form a new government.

Lack of confidence and trust in the British prime minister Boris Johnson eventually led to his resignation and removal as head of his party.

PEOPLE AND POLITICS

In June 2022, the UK's Conservative party issued a vote of no confidence against their leader, Boris Johnson. Johnson won the vote but his position was greatly weakened by over 40 percent of his party voting against him. A month later, the resignation of many government ministers and staff led to Johnson's own resignation as Conservative leader, although he continued as prime minister until a successor, Liz Truss, was found two months later.

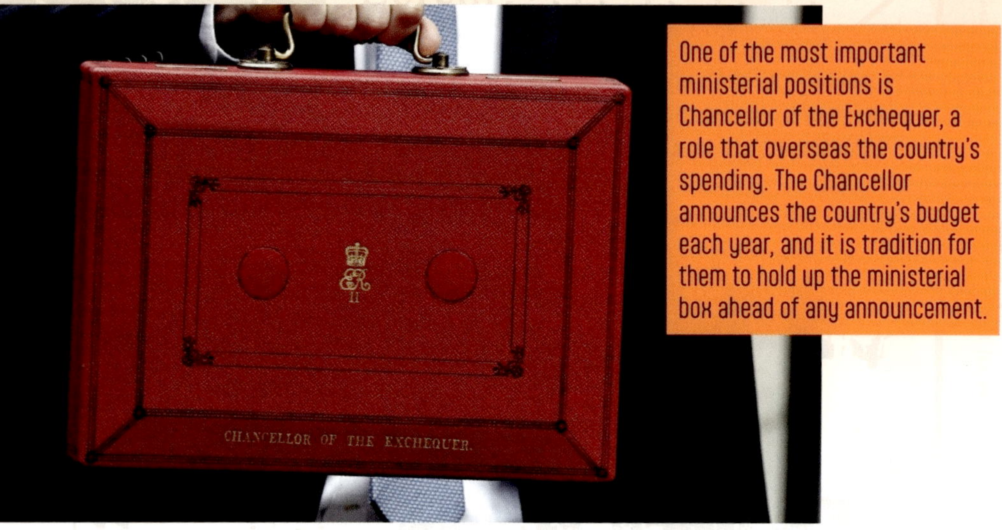

One of the most important ministerial positions is Chancellor of the Exchequer, a role that overseas the country's spending. The Chancellor announces the country's budget each year, and it is tradition for them to hold up the ministerial box ahead of any announcement.

A Cabinet of Ministers

At the center of the UK government is the cabinet. The cabinet is made up of ministers chosen by the prime minister from members of parliament. There are around 20 ministers in the UK cabinet. They are senior members of the government who meet weekly with the prime minister to discuss important issues.

Heading up Departments

The prime minister also chooses people to head up departments and agencies of the government, such as the Department for Education (DfE). There are around 100 ministers who are responsible for more than 40 departments. Government employees, called civil servants, do the day-to-day running of the departments, but it is the ministers who make sure policies are properly put in place and carried through.

Other Bodies

In the UK government, there are more than 300 agencies and other public bodies that need to be run. Not all these departments, agencies, and public bodies are run by ministers though—civil servants run some of them.

A Deputy to Help

Also supporting the prime minister is a deputy prime minister. This person may head different committees in the government and help build relationships with other countries. The deputy prime minister is also kept fully briefed at all times so they can also take over the role of leadership, if needed, in the prime minister's absence.

Parliamentary Government in Action

The role of prime minister is a very important one. The person in this role leads the country through good and bad times. Former British prime minister Margaret Thatcher (1925–2013) is one of the most famous British prime ministers. Read the following *Wall Street Journal* quote about her, which was written after she died:

> "Mrs Thatcher is remembered within Britain mostly for her role in revolutionizing the fading economy, in a process that caused huge social change and division, and for the successful retaking of the Falkland Islands, the British South Atlantic territory invaded by Argentina in 1982—after which she declared, 'We have ceased to be a nation in retreat.' In Europe, she is remembered as a prickly leader who thrived on confrontation, but who ultimately agreed to foster some of the European Union's most significant developments ..."

After reading this quote, what have you learned about the role of prime minister?

PAST AND PRESENT:

What have you learned about the former prime minister Margaret Thatcher?

Do you think a prime minister like Margaret Thatcher would be popular in the UK today? Give reasons for your answer.

Margaret Thatcher

A Typical Parliament

The House of Commons and the House of Lords are the two legislative bodies that make up the parliament in the UK. It is typical of a bicameral parliament to have both an upper and lower legislative house.

The Upper House

Members of the House of Lords in the UK parliament are not elected, but are appointed by the monarch, following recommendations from a special committee called the House of Lords Appointments Commission. The prime minister also suggests people for the house. There are three types of members: life peers, bishops, and elected hereditary peers. The hereditary peers are the equivalent of the noblemen who sat in the Great Council of the medieval period.

The Lower House

Members of the House of Commons in the UK parliament, known as MPs, are elected by the people and each represents a certain political party. There can be as many as 10 different parties represented in the house, and each has different values and goals for government.

Three Main Parties

The three main political parties in the UK are the Conservatives, Labour, and Liberal Democrats. These parties are represented in both the House of Commons and the House of Lords. After an election, if a party wins over half the seats in parliament, it gains a majority and takes control of parliament. The prime minister is chosen from this party. The main party in the minority becomes the opposition party. It debates proposals for new laws, known as bills, put forward by the majority party. The opposition party also submits its own bills for consideration by the majority party.

Three main political parties dominate British politics.

Parliamentary Government in Action

Sometimes, no single political party gains a majority vote. This is called a "hung parliament." It happened in the UK in 2010 when the leading Conservative Party only won 36 percent of the vote. To move forward, a coalition government was formed between the Conservatives and the Liberal Democrats. The Conservative leader, David Cameron, became prime minister, while the Liberal Democrat leader, Nick Clegg, became deputy prime minister.

Why do you think a majority vote is needed for a government to rule effectively?

What do you think are the advantages and disadvantages of a coalition government?"

PAST AND PRESENT:

Coalition governments were formed in the UK during World War I (1914–1918) and World War II (1939–1945) to steer the country through challenging times. Can you think of other global events in the future that might benefit from a shared form of government?

Sir Winston Churchill (1874–1965) led as prime minister of the coalition government of wartime Britain in the 1940s.

The Process of Making Laws

A parliamentary government must adapt to the needs of its changing country. To make changes, new laws must be created. They are debated in a parliament, where they are called bills. Once passed, these bills become laws. Here is how a bill becomes a law in the UK parliament.

Drafting a Bill

First, a government department makes a draft bill. Next, different committees in the Commons or Lords, or joint committees involving both houses, review the bill and then make changes before it is introduced to parliament. Sometimes, they issue papers about the bills for the public to read and provide responses.

Known as Green Papers

These consultation documents are usually called Green Papers. That is because historically they were printed on green paper to separate them from other types of government documents. Once the draft bill is fully approved, it can be presented to parliament.

PEOPLE AND POLITICS

When David Cameron resigned as Britain's prime minister in 2016, he had served 15 years in various forms of political office—six years as prime minister, 15 years as MP for Witney, 11 years as leader of the Conservative party, and five years as leader of the opposition. In 2023, Cameron was appointed foreign secretary. He was no longer an elected MP, but was given a seat in the House of Lords, because it's customary for ministers to be chosen from the legislature.

David Cameron

A Need to Agree

A bill is presented to parliament by the government, an MP or Lord, or a private individual or organization. It can either be presented before the House of Commons or the House of Lords. Once presented, the bill can then be properly debated. After it is examined and discussed, changes, or amendments, can be made. The House of Commons and the House of Lords both need to agree on the bill's content. Then the amended bill is sent to the monarch.

Needing Approval

The monarch must give each new bill their approval. This is called Royal Assent. The Assent can be given either directly by the monarch or by someone acting on their behalf. Once a bill has the Royal Assent, it becomes an Act of Parliament and is a law. The law can then be put into effect by the relevant government department. For example, a law about roads would be the responsibility of the Department for Transport (DfT). A law about education would be the responsibility of the Department for Education (DfE). If a law needs to be changed later, another Act must be passed by parliament before that change of law can happen.

Although parliament passes a bill, it can only become law with the king's approval. Since becoming king, Charles has made changes to the process of Royal Assent to make the system speedier and more efficient.

The Core Value

In any democratic system, the core value is that the people are fully involved with the government of their country. People of different areas, called constituencies, choose who represents them in the government. It is then the job of those elected officials to represent the desires and needs of all the people in their constituencies.

Holding Elections

In the UK parliament, the House of Commons is the elected body of the government, and MPs are the elected representatives. Every five years, the House of Commons is dissolved. This means that every seat becomes vacant and a new House of Commons must be formed. To fill the seats, elections are held. If an MP retires, or dies, a single election, called a by-election, takes place in that constituency to find a new representative for that area.

Parliamentary Government in Action

Israel has a long history of political struggles. After Israeli prime minister Yitzhak Rabin was assassinated in 1995, a new law was passed that allowed the prime minister to be directly elected by the people. The result was a kind of hybrid parliament, with elements of the presidential system. This elected minister still relies heavily on the support of the parliament, though.

Why do you think Israel changed to an elected prime minister?

Do you see any problems or advantages in this hybrid system?

In Israel, the prime minister is voted for directly by the people.

A Choice of Candidate

Each voter has a choice of candidates for their constituency. The candidates come from different political parties or run as an independent, meaning they do not belong to any party. All candidates must pay a fee, called a deposit, to take part, which is then returned to them if they receive more than 5 percent of the votes. The candidate who receives the most votes becomes the MP for that constituency. In the House of Commons, the political party that gains over half the seats in parliament, takes control of the house. In the UK, there are 650 constituencies, each represented in the House of Commons. There is an average of 68,175 voters in each constituency.

Benjamin Netanyahu

PEOPLE AND POLITICS

In 1996, at the age of 47, Benjamin Netanyahu became Israel's youngest prime minister and the first to be elected by popular vote. More than 25 years later, in 2022, he was reelected for a sixth term—more than any other prime minister in the country's history—having served between 1996–1999 and 2009–2021. Netanyahu's promise to keep Israel safe brought him popularity, although his rule has become controversial with some people in recent years.

King Charles III and his wife Queen Camilla (center) met with German president Frank-Walter Steinmeier and his wife in 2023.

Steeped in Ceremony

Some of the more colorful parts of the UK parliament are its ceremonies and traditions. When the king opens a new session of parliament, he wears silks, furs, and a jewel-encrusted crown. The royal carriages and horses carry him from his home Buckingham Palace to the Houses of Parliament. This is the pomp and ceremony of parliament and some of its great traditions date back many centuries.

A State Visit

When the leader from another country comes to the UK to formally represent the interests of their country, or the king makes a visit abroad, it's called a State Visit. This leader will meet the king, who entertains them at a State Banquet. These banquets are often held at Buckingham Palace and are grand affairs that involve weeks of preparation. About 150 guests are usually invited to State Banquets and the king will usually make a speech before dinner. The king sometimes makes a speech before both Houses of Parliament during the visit.

Opening Parliament

The ceremony that gets the most attention is the State Opening of Parliament. It starts the session of parliament for the year. It is the king's duty to open the session. He travels to Westminster Palace in a horse-drawn carriage. This part of the ceremony is often very colorful and dramatic, with the king traveling in a stunning carriage through the streets of London accompanied by the Household Cavalry Mounted Regiment and other members of the armed forces. Huge crowds gather to watch the king's journey and television crews broadcast the event to audiences around the world.

A Symbolic Moment

The ceremony takes place in the House of Lords, where the king sits on his throne. Then the members of the House of Commons are summoned to the event. The king then delivers a speech to the two houses. It outlines parliament's goals and plans for the year. This speech is just ceremonial, however. The government writes and approves the points of the speech before the ceremony. While the opening of parliament is symbolic only, it displays some of the more exciting and dramatic aspects of the UK government.

PEOPLE AND POLITICS

In 2023, King Charles III took part in his first State Opening of Parliament since becoming king, although he'd stood in for his mother the previous year due to her poor health. King Charles and his wife, Queen Camilla, traveled to Westminster in the Diamond Jubilee State Coach, where Charles received the Imperial State Crown and the Robe of State. The State Opening began with a ceremonial search of the cellars in the Houses of Parliament by the King's bodyguard to commemorate Guy Fawkes' "gunpowder plot" of 1605. Members of the House of Commons then joined to listen to Charles deliver his speech from the throne in the House of Lords.

Before he himself became monarch, Charles took on the responsibility of opening parliament for his late mother, Queen Elizabeth, when she was unable to do so.

CHAPTER 3

Living with Parliaments

On Canada Day, thousands of Canadians visit Parliament Hill, in Ottawa, to celebrate the country's birthday on July 1. They wear red and white, like the colors of the country's flag. Ceremonies and performances fill the day, and the celebration ends with fireworks. This is a day of the year that Canadians show their national pride.

Fireworks on Canada Day, 1 July

Involving the People

Life in a country with a parliamentary government involves the people of the country. Their votes decide who runs their country. To best represent the people, a country's residents must be involved with their political system. In Canada's 2021 general election, 62 percent of the people voted. Other countries with parliamentary systems have higher turnouts, however. Norway gets around 77 percent of its voters to participate in elections. Around 78 percent of New Zealand's people voted during elections in 2023.

Expressing Opinions

It is important in a parliamentary system that people express their opinions. A vote expresses a resident's opinion and directly affects what bills will be supported in a parliament. In turn, the laws that pass then directly affect residents of a country. Residents are not always happy about the laws that are passed by a parliament. If a constituency is unhappy about a new law, its people can express that opinion to their representative. The representative can then try to affect change in parliament on their behalf.

Parliamentary Government in Action

Canada is a constitutional monarchy as well as a parliamentary democracy, whereby the sovereign—Britain's King Charles III—is the Head of State. On a day-to-day basis, however, the sovereign's role is carried out by the governor general, who acts on behalf of the sovereign, not only in Canada but also abroad. The governor general is appointed by the king on the advice of Canada's prime minister and usually holds the office for five years.

Why is the role of Canada's governor general so important?

Why do you think Canada's prime minister advises on a suitable candidate?

PEOPLE AND POLITICS

In 2015, Justin Trudeau became Canada's second-youngest prime minister when he was elected at the age of 43. He was first elected to the House of Commons in 2008, and followed in the footsteps of his charismatic father, the late Pierre Trudeau, who served as Canada's prime minister from 1968–1979 and 1980–1984, and leader of the opposition in the intervening years. As leader of the Liberal Party, Justin's election ended nearly a decade of Conservative rule.

Justin Trudeau

Parliament in the Media

Access to information and openness are key aspects of parliamentary governments. They are held accountable to the people of their countries. Most parliamentary chambers have public galleries where people can watch debates take place. Otherwise, they can find out what is going on in a parliament from traditional media, such as newspapers and television, or they gather information from the Internet.

Posted Before Voting

In many countries, bills are publicly posted for all to read before a vote is taken. Debates of bills may be videotaped and then posted online. And vote counts are published too. Knowing what a government is doing is very important in democratic countries. It keeps the people involved with their representatives and the decisions that they make.

Information to the People

The media is one method of getting that information out to the people. Unlike some countries, such as those run by a dictatorship, where the leaders will limit what the public can find out, in parliamentary countries the government does not control the media. Instead, the media independently reports on the news of the government. Traditionally, the news of the government has been reported through television, newspapers, and websites. Today, social media has changed the way news is reported to the people, and political parties have adapted to that.

Social media has become one of the key channels through which we communicate about politics.

Social Sharing

In recent years, people have been able to get almost instant access to the news through social media. People in different countries want to have this direct access to their government. A few countries have issued formal policies on how government should use social media, such as X, Instagram, and Facebook. The Canadian government encourages departments to use social media. The UK parliament encourages members to use X to respond to the public's policy questions. With all forms of media, parliaments today aim to accurately and openly share the news of the government.

Parliamentary Government in Action

In the months leading up to the 2016 US presidential election, Donald Trump managed to gain unprecedented public attention thanks to his use of social media, such as Facebook advertising, helping him reach far more voters than traditional political means. Then, during his presidency, Trump's use of X enabled him to connect personally with his supporters, to respond to his opponents, and to outline policy plans. Trump could engage directly with the public, rather than allowing the media to represent his views, greatly increasing his influence and his ability to command attention.

Donald Trump heavily used social media in his presidential campaign and after, once he had been elected to power.

CHAPTER 4

Pros and Cons of Parliamentary Systems

Parliamentary governments give people an opportunity to makes changes in the world. In 2013, for example, India's population were angry that law enforcement was doing nothing to prevent crimes against women. Thousands of people protested, and India's parliament responded. A bill passed quickly that imposed tougher penalties against attackers. In 2023, women in India were also given a fairer voice, when new legislation improved the political representation of women in parliament, following campaigns from many women's rights groups.

One Benefit

A benefit of the parliamentary system is that it can quickly pass bills into laws. This is because the executive (governing) powers and the legislative (law-making) powers are fused together. They work together as one voice speaking for the people. This is unlike the presidential system, where the executive and legislative bodies are separate. They do not always have the same opinion, adding conflict and delaying the passage of certain bills.

Indian politician and member of parliament, Diya Kumari, addresses a public meeting in Rajasthan

An Abuse of Power

Throughout history, there are many governments and leaders who have abused their power. Corruption is a huge problem. Some leaders use their powers in government for personal gains. They may, perhaps, steal funds meant to help the people. They may take bribes to pass bills that may not be in the best interest of the public. A report by the World Bank, an organization set up in 1944 to help developing countries, studied corruption and political systems. It found that parliaments and democracies have fewer instances of corruption than other types of government. The World Bank continues to work to build transparency and accountability in government institutions around the world.

Parliamentary Government in Action

In 2018, the leader of Spain's Podemos Party said on X: "Democracy can't tolerate criminals in charge of government." He was responding to Spain's worst-ever political corruption scandal in which businessmen had bribed Spanish politicians with money to gain government contracts. Those involved were convicted of fraud and lost their government positions. Spain's prime minister at the time, Mariano Rajoy, also announced his resignation following a vote of no confidence.

PEOPLE AND POLITICS

Alexandria Ocasio-Cortez became the youngest woman to serve in the US Congress when she was elected in 2018 at the age of 29. Originally a political outsider, Alexandria used social media to gather support and relied on small financial contributions toward her campaign—nearly 62 percent of her $2 million funds came from small individual contributions under $200. She made the point that she wanted to win for her views rather than because she'd taken money from big companies and rich people, and it was a winning formula.

Alexandria Ocasio-Cortez

Problems with Parliaments

In the parliamentary system, voters cannot directly choose a prime minister, who is the chief executive. Some think this is the main difficulty with a parliamentary system, as the person who is the head of government is not directly accountable to a country's people. This is unlike the system in the United States, where the people must vote their head of government, the American president, into office.

Different Systems

In the presidential system, if the executive powers do not agree with a bill, it most likely will not pass. In the parliamentary system, if the majority party wants a bill to pass, it will pass. The exception is when certain members of that party disagree with a proposed law and vote against the government. With the presidential system, there are more checks and balances in the legislative (law-making) process. This means that bills are examined separately by legislative and executive powers. If the house, senate, or executive powers do not agree with a bill it most likely will not pass.

Doing Things Differently

Some countries believe their parliaments need to do things differently. In 2024, thousands of people gathered near the Hungarian parliament in Budapest, calling for the resignation of their prime minister, Viktor Orbán, following accusations of corruption. Just a month earlier, crowds of people gathered near the Slovakian parliament in Bratislava, to protest against the way the prime minister, Robert Fico, was dealing with crime and corruption. Meanwhile, political instability in Italy has led to frequent changes of government. All these instances are just a few of the issues facing parliamentary systems.

Protestors on the streets of Budapest, Hungary, in 2024

Parliamentary Government in Action

In 2022, Italy swore in its seventieth government in 77 years. The country has had, on average, a new government every 13 months. Italy has a large number of political parties, making it difficult for any one party to secure a majority in parliament.

What do you think are the advantages and disadvantages of multiple political parties?

If small political parties form a coalition, do you think this is a good or a bad thing for parliamentary democracy? Give reasons for your views.

Recent challenges such as the war in Ukraine have divided public opinion in Italy. How do you think challenges like these impact the results of elections?

Italian politician, Giorgia Meloni, is shown here campaigning in 2021. In 2022, Meloni became Italy's first woman prime minster.

CHAPTER 5

The Future of Parliaments

Parliamentary systems of government are spreading. When countries decide to become democracies and need to form new governments, many are choosing a parliamentary system. These parliaments run into similar issues around the world but are supported in their transition to democracy.

New Governments

Several countries have recently adopted governments with parliamentary executives. The citizens of Burkina Faso had their first free and fair elections in 2015 to elect a president after almost three decades of one-man rule. Myanmar (Burma) in Southeast Asia changed to a parliamentary system in January 2011, but it wasn't until 2016 that citizens were able to vote for their first president, Htin Kyaw, after over five decades of military rule.

Htin Kyaw meets Indian prime minister, Narendra Modi, in 2017

Joining Governments

The Inter-Parliamentary Union (IPU) is an organization, founded in 1889, that links different parliaments together. Its members are made up of more than 180 national parliaments, including the UK, Germany, Japan, Pakistan, Uganda, Sierra Leone, Venezuela, and Finland.

Setting the Standard

The IPU sets standards for world parliaments. It helps new parliaments. It helps countries emerging from conflicts to set up new democratic systems. It serves as a place where members of parliaments can meet and discuss issues within their government systems. The IPU works to promote democracy, peace, sustainable development, human rights, women in politics, and education, science, and culture. It also tracks parliaments and their elections around the world.

Connections Solve Probems

As the world becomes increasingly connected, the IPU helps governments work together to solve world problems. Knowing how one parliament has dealt with an issue may help another country to deal with similar issues.

Parliamentary Government in Action

Tunisia established a new parliament in 2011 after the overthrow of President Zine al-Abidine Ben Ali, who had ruled the country as a one-party state for 23 years. Political parties agreed to work together to promote democracy and drafted a new constitution, but it was difficult to reach agreements and no party was able to gain a majority vote in government. After a decade of slow economic growth, the country is seeing more authoritarian measures again. In 2021, President Saied dissolved parliament and in 2022 he won a referendum allowing him to introduce a new constitution, lessening the powers of the parliament and the judiciary.

Why do you think Tunisia struggled to adapt to a parliamentary democracy?

What impact do you think the economy has on the way people vote and what they want from their government?

Tunisians show support for their president, Kais Saied, in 2022

Parliaments and Women

Women have a bright future in parliaments. An IPU study found that the number of women in parliaments worldwide is increasing. In 2022, women took 26.5 percent of parliamentary seats. There were more women in the lower houses of parliaments than in the upper houses. The country with the highest percentage of women in parliament was Rwanda, in Africa, where women held 61.3 percent of the seats in the country's lower house.

Working for Greater Equality

The IPU's Forum of Women Parliamentarians was set up in 1978 and works to improve the political representation of women in national parliaments. It provides an opportunity for women to learn about the work of other countries in addressing gender inequality, and to work together with ideas and solutions. Around 200 MPs attend their meetings, and male MPs contribute to the Forum's work, showing that working toward gender equality is a shared responsibility. Thanks to the work of the Forum, any parliament with women members must now include at least one woman in meetings for votes to be counted.

PEOPLE AND POLITICS

Many women have also been great leaders of parliaments. Margaret Thatcher was the first female prime minister in the UK parliament. She held that position between 1979 and 1990, making her the longest-serving British prime minister of the twentieth century. Indira Gandhi was India's prime minister for more than 11 years, from 1966 to 1977, and then again from 1980 until she was assassinated in 1984. Julia Gillard became the first female Australian prime minister in 2010 and in New Zealand in 2017, Jacinda Ardern became the country's youngest prime minister for more than 150 years. Ardern served for five years, steering New Zealand through some of its most challenging times, including a terrorist attack, a deadly volcanic eruption, and the COVID-19 pandemic.

Jacinda Ardern

There are greater opportunities than ever for young women who want to enter politics and parliament. As more women serve in parliaments, they become better systems of government. With women involved, parliaments more equally represent the people of the countries they serve.

Parliamentary Government in Action

In 2015, members of the United Nations (UN) set out a series of 17 Sustainable Development Goals to help achieve a better and more sustainable future for all. Goal 5 is to "achieve gender equality and empower all women and girls." This includes an end to discrimination, exploitation, and inequalities of opportunity.

Why do you think women face barriers to positions of political leadership?

What stereotypes might influence the way people view a male or female political candidate?

What barriers might prevent women taking part in the electoral process?

CONCLUSION

Parliamentary Government Past, Present, and Future

The parliamentary system has been around for centuries. This old form of government still thrives today in countries around the world. It is a democratic government that works only if the people of the country are involved. Through elections, representatives become members of parliament. They then represent the voters in their constituencies.

Monarchy or Republic

We have seen that a parliamentary system can be either a constitutional monarchy or a republic. If it is a constitutional monarchy, a monarch is the head of state. If it is a republic, a president is the head of state. The heads of state for both types of systems are ceremonial and usually do not have any political powers. The head of government in parliaments is chosen from the majority political party in the assembly. This person is responsible to, and dependent upon, the support of parliament.

Regular free and fair elections help to keep parliamentary government working at its best.

Quick to Make Laws

Parliaments are known for their quick passage of bills into laws. They also work readily with social media such as Facebook to share the information about their legislative work. Women are also an increasing presence in parliaments. With a union of world parliaments, information and assistance is shared with both developing and more experienced parliaments. This old governmental system has adapted to a changing world. It is a political system that is sure to endure into the future.

Parliamentary Government in Action

Edmund Burke (c. 1729–1797) was an Irish-born member of the UK parliament in the late eighteenth century. He warned against the corruption of parliaments, stating in 1774:

> "Parliament is not a congress of ambassadors from different and hostile interests; which interests each must maintain, as an agent and advocate, against other agents and advocates; but parliament is a deliberative assembly of one nation, with one interest, that of the whole; where, not local purposes, not local prejudices, ought to guide, but the general good, resulting from the general reason of the whole."

What do you think Burke meant by this statement?

Do you agree or disagree with his philosophy?

From what you have learned, do you think Burke's words represent how parliamentary government works in practice?

Edmund Burke

Glossary

Act a bill that has been passed by the legislature
affirmation the action of stating something as a fact
assembly a group of people who have been elected to make a country's laws
bicameral having two branches
bill a written plan for a new law
cabinet a group of advisors for the head of a country's government
ceremonial a role involving little to no actual power
ceremony the formal actions carried out on an important occasion
colonies territories that have been settled by people from another country
Commonwealth an association that includes the UK and countries or states that were once part of the British Empire; the British monarch is the head of state for members of the Commonwealth
constituency a group of voters in an area that elects a representative for a legislative body
constitution a set of rules and principles that lays down how a nation should be governed
constitutional monarchy a monarchy in which the power of the monarch is limited by a constitution
democracy a system in which the government is voted for by most or all the adults in that country
dissolved to close or dismiss
election the process of selecting someone or deciding something by voting
executive the branch of government that creates policy and carries it out
judiciary the branch of government consisting of the judges and law courts
legislative having the power to make laws for a country
legislature the branch of government that debates policy and makes laws
majority the greater number
media the newspapers, radio, television, and other forms of communication
minister a person who is elected to help govern a country
minority the lesser number
monarchy rule by a king or queen, who usually inherits their role
noblemen important and wealthy landowners who had great power
opposition a group that resists the majority
peer a member of the nobility, or a bishop
permission telling a person or organization that they are allowed to do something they want to do
political party a group of people with similar ideas about how a country should be run
pomp ceremony and magnificent display

representative a person chosen to act on behalf of a larger group

republic a democracy where the head of state is also elected, rather than a hereditary monarch

revolutionizing making dramatic and far-reaching changes to something

symbolic serving as a symbol of something

unicameral having a single legislative house

vacant a position that is not filled

Find Out More

Books

Foster, Jeff. *For Which We Stand: How Our Government Works and Why It Matters*. Scholastic, 2020.

Political Science for Kids: Presidential vs Parliamentary Systems of Government. Baby Professor, 2017.

Sheehan, Ben. *What Does the Constitution Say? A Kid's Guide to How Our Democracy Works*. Black Dog & Leventhal, 2021.

Websites

Learn more about the work and role of the UK parliament in this video:
learning.parliament.uk/en/resources/introduction-to-parliament-primary-video

Find out more about how the UK parliament works at:
www.gov.uk/government/how-government-works

Some useful games and videos about democracy and parliamentary government can be found at:
www.neok12.com/Democracy.htm

Index

ABOUT THE AUTHOR

Alex Webb has written many children's books and has a particular interest in history and politics. She has found researching and writing this book fascinating and hopes that it helps students everywhere gain knowledge and insight into political systems and how they work.